dos
ook

Contents

About Barbados 1

Facts on Barbados 3

Some Facts on Barbados Rum 6

The Story of Barbados Rum 9

History of Hanschell/Cockspur 19

Rum Based Drinks

- Daiquiri 21
- Cocktails 23
- Fruit and Rum 26
- Highballs 28
- Juleps 30
- Pina Colada 32
- Punches 34
- Rum and One 37
- White Rum 39
- Hot Rum 41

Cooking with Rum 44

About Barbados

'Barbados is different'. This is the opinion of most visitors to the island, and it is shared by the inhabitants of the neighbouring islands. Wherein lies the difference and to what can we attribute it?

Though Barbados is always regarded as being within the Caribbean, in fact it stands out in the Atlantic, a hundred miles east of the chain of small islands encircling the Caribbean Sea. Unlike its neighbours, it is a coral island and relatively flat; the land rises gradually in a series of terraces to 1,100 feet. The quarter of a million people who inhabit its 166 square miles make it one of the most densely populated countries in the world. It is blessed with a nearly ideal climate and, because of the coral reefs which surround it, with excellent beaches.

The visitor arriving by air or by sea will be surprised by the high standard of the airport and harbour facilities. He will quickly discover that other services are provided and maintained to the same standard. As he travels round the island, he will be impressed by the importance attached to social services

such as health and education, by the dense network of roads and the heavy expenditure on road improvement, by the fact that almost all available land is under cultivation, and by views so unexpected that they take one's breath away. When he gets to know the island better, he will be struck by the political maturity of its people.

Barbados was an uninhabited island covered with dense forest when it was settled by the English in 1627. Twenty years later its population far exceeded that of any English-speaking island in the area.

Barbados is the only West Indian island that has never been in foreign hands. Because of the importation of African slaves on a vast scale in the seventeenth and eighteenth centuries, the population today is preponderantly Negro, but until well into the present century all political and economic power was exercised by the small white minority. Fortunately, respect for political traditions was deep-rooted, and this ensured that the transfer of power from one section of the population to the other would be gradual and smooth. The achievement of political independence in 1966 had little effect on the life of the community.

Today Barbados is an independent state within the Commonwealth. The Queen of England is Queen of Barbados and is represented by a Governor General, whose functions are almost entirely ceremonial. As in England, there is a Prime Minister and Cabinet and a bi-cameral legislature.

Facts on Barbados

Barbados
The island was named Los Barbudos (the bearded ones) in a Spanish document of 1511. The most popular theory is that the name came from the aerial roots of the bearded fig tree, which is still to be found in the island.

Location
The most easterly of the Caribbean islands. Only 4½ hours by jet from New York, 5 hours from Toronto and 8½ hours from London.

Description
A pear-shaped island, 21 miles long by 14 miles wide, containing everything a vacationer could want. Hilly but not mountainous

– the highest point is Mount Hillaby, 1,105 feet above sea level. The island is formed mainly of coral and is bounded by miles of white sand beaches. The Atlantic side, the north east, is rugged and picturesque with the large Atlantic breakers pounding the beaches. On the west side the sea is calm and tranquil for safe bathing.

Climate
Healthy and pleasant with bright sun for most days of the year. Although tropical, constant sea breezes ensure that the heat is rarely uncomfortable.

Capital
Bridgetown on the south-west coast. It is also the commercial centre and port and the home of the Barbados parliament.

Government
Barbados is an independent nation and a member of the British Commonwealth. Government is based on the Westminster model and fully democratic. Parliament consists of two houses. The lower house, the House of Assembly, consists of 27 members elected by the people. The upper house, the Senate, consists of 21 appointed members. Barbados enjoys universal adult suffrage with the voting age at 18 years.

Population
The population is approximately 250,000, making Barbados one of the most densely populated areas in the world with 1,506 to the square mile. Approximately 90% are of Afro-West Indian origin with the rest white or of mixed race.

Language
English is the language of Barbados and it is commonly spoken with a very distinctive dialect.

Industry
Apart from tourism the main industry is sugar cane from which sugar, molasses and Barbados fine rum are produced. There is also a wide range of small light industries.

Education
Barbados has an excellent education system which is widely

admired. Education in Government schools is free and all children enjoy secondary schooling. In addition to the primary and secondary schools, the system includes a Teacher Training College, Community College, Polytechnic, Technical Institute, Homecraft Centre, Hotel School, Evening Institute and a branch of the University of the West Indies.

Currency
The Barbados dollar is worth approximately two to one U.S. dollar. U.S. dollars are widely accepted, although most goods are priced in local dollars.

Brief History
1627, first English settlers landed at Holetown; 1639, first Parliament established; 1651, island besieged by British forces; 1652, Articles of Capitulation agreed at Oistins; 1834, slavery abolished; 1881, Executive Committee formed; 1944, women allowed to vote; 1951, adult suffrage; 1954, Ministerial Government introduced; 1957, Cabinet Government; 1966, independence within the Commonwealth; 1966, member of the United Nations.

Some Facts on Barbados Rum

Rum Distilleries

Until the end of the nineteenth century all Barbados rum was made on sugar plantations in stills adjacent to the sugar mills. Today, the island's two distilleries are owned by companies which are entirely independent of the sugar industry. One of them, Mount Gay, makes rum only for sale under its own brand name. The other, The West India Rum Refinery, sells all its rum to dealers and has no brand name of its own. The distilleries buy molasses from a company which markets all the molasses made by the Barbados Sugar Industry.

Originally all rum was made in pot stills. In the simplest form of pot still a batch of fermented molasses, known as 'wash', is heated to produce a distillate. Today this distillate is redistilled and pot still rum is also called double-distilled rum. Pot still rum is now generally used in small proportions blended with other rum made in continuous stills to impart flavour.

The continuous still rum is produced continuously instead of in batches and the still can make a rum which is much lighter in flavour. Many distilleries make both light and heavy rum in continuous stills, but in Barbados all the heavier flavouring rum is made in pot stills.

Maturing and Ageing of Rum
Very light rum made in a continuous still is often drunk after being kept only a short time in barrels. Most people agree that continuous still rum continues to improve with ageing, at least up to ten years. There is general agreement that pot still rums and the heavier rums made in the continuous still should be aged for longer periods than lighter rums. A five-year-old rum is very good and a ten-year-old rum is mellower and even better.

Barbados rum is matured in American white oak barrels which hold approximately 40 liquid imperial gallons (48 liquid wine gallons). Before the rum is put into barrels, its strength is reduced by adding water. Within limits, the lower the strength at which it is matured, the better the quality of the rum after a given period. The wood of the barrels acts on the rum so as to give it smoothness and mellowness.

Colour of Rum
All rum is white when it is distilled. If it is put into barrels, it acquires colour from the wood. As the intensity of the colour can vary slightly from barrel to barrel and according to the length of time it is in the barrel, most bottlers add a small amount of caramel, when necessary, to ensure that all their rum is uniform in colour. The more caramel that is added, the darker the rum. A matured rum can have the colour removed by filtering it through carbon.

Which rums were used in the rum ration of the Royal Navy?
The rum ration of the Royal Navy was a blend of rums from several countries, one of which was Barbados. By tradition it was very dark rum, and it therefore contained a lot of caramel.

Differences in Rum
It was always considered that rums made in different sugar-producing countries had their own peculiar characteristics and,

within the Caribbean, Barbados rum has always enjoyed much popularity. Today most countries are making rums in their continuous stills which are so neutral that the difference in taste of very light rums made in different countries is small. But when this very light rum is blended with heavier rums, the difference between the blends of one country and another is still detectable. The reasons for the differences are not fully understood.

Obvious factors that contribute to it are climate, soil, water and perhaps the methods of preparing the molasses wash and the manufacturing techniques.

Rum Blending

Blending means the mixing of two or more different sorts of rum, with possibly the addition of other flavouring matter. In some sugar-producing countries several different types of rum from the same still may be included in a blend. In Barbados a blend contains rum from a continuous still and rum from a pot still. Apart from additives (which in Barbados are used extremely sparingly), what mainly determines the difference between one blend and another is the percentage of each ingredient, the age of the different ingredients (i.e. the length of time they have been in barrels) and the strength at which they have been matured.

The Story of Barbados Rum

A Spirit from the Sugar Cane

Rum is a spirit. What distinguishes it from other spirits, such as whisky, gin and brandy, is that it is obtained by distilling either the juice extracted from the sugar cane or, more commonly, from molasses, which is the thick, dark brown liquid which is left after as much sugar as possible has been extracted from the sugar cane juice.

Rum of a sort may have been made for almost as long as sugar cane has been cultivated, perhaps for 2,000 years. It is in Asia that we first hear of sugar cane cultivation. It spread to North Africa, and from there to Sicily and Spain, and by 1420 the Portuguese were growing it in Madeira.

Christopher Columbus introduced sugar cane into the West Indies, and in the sixteenth century the Spaniards were making sugar on a large scale in Hispaniola, Cuba and Puerto Rico. We are told that, initially at least, though the fermented juice of the cane was drunk, there was no distillation of the skimmings or molasses. Some of the molasses was fed to the labourers and livestock but most of it was thrown away. We can assume, however, that by the end of the century a distilled spirit of a sort was being produced, though probably only for local consumption.

Meanwhile the Portuguese had established settlements in Brazil. They brought sugar cane plants from Madeira and they developed the manufacture of sugar into a flourishing industry, with Pernambuco and Bahia as the most important centres of production. Before long they were fermenting the molasses and distilling it to produce a spirit. It had a dreadful taste and the Portuguese themselves would not touch it, but it was drunk by the native Indians and the African slaves.

It was not until the seventeenth century that the English, the French and the Dutch began to colonize the small islands of the eastern Caribbean. A few years after the establishment of a settlement in St Kitts, the English sent settlers to the uninhabited

island of Barbados, which quickly became the most highly populated and the most important English colony in the area. At first its main export crops were tobacco and cotton, but by the middle 1630s one or two enterprising planters began looking for a crop which would bring better returns. They experimented with sugar cane. They found it ideally suited to the soil and climatic conditions and they went to Pernambuco in Brazil, which was then in the hands of the Dutch, to learn the technique of sugar manufacture. Soon after 1640 they were producing sugar of an acceptable quality and they were distilling a product from the skimmings of the copper kettles and from the molasses.

The Spirit is Named 'Rum'

In 1647 Richard Ligon arrived in Barbados, a Royalist refugee from the English Civil War. He spent three years in the island and he wrote a book about it. In this book he gives a detailed description, illustrated by drawings, of the whole process of the manufacture of sugar and the distillation of the cane spirit.

Ligon has to admit that the spirit made in Barbados in his time had an unpleasant taste and it seems that it was not then drunk by those who could afford something better. It was very strong, and those who imbibed quickly felt its effects; as Ligon puts it, 'it lays them asleep on the ground'. Christian servants were given a dram or two to refresh them after sweating in the sun for ten hours a day and it was regularly prescribed for slaves suffering from 'any weakness or decay in their spirits or stomach'.

At two shillings and sixpence a gallon, the spirit sold well. It was bought by planters who did not have their own sugar works, the taverns must have been good customers and it was sold to ships, both for consumption by the crews and for re-sale overseas. Ligon says that a planter who owned a still – and there were plenty of them – could make thirty pounds sterling a week. This must have represented sales in the island of not less than 200,000 gallons a year and this figure does not include the large quantities consumed by servants and slaves. It is not surprising that some of the other islands soon began to make this spirit.

Ligon always refers to the spirit as kill-devil which aptly describes the properties of the drink. The name was still in use in Barbados in the nineteenth century for the raw white rum which caused so much drunkenness among the British troops who garrisoned the island. The name was too much of a colloquialism to be accorded official recognition and even in 1651 an Act of the Legislature still refers to 'this country's spirits'. By this time, however, a new name had become current. A person (his identity is unknown) who must have arrived in the island just about the time of Ligon's departure (April 1650) has left us a description of the island. He tells us that 'the chiefe fudling they make in the Island is Rumbullion, alias Kill Divill, and this is made of suggar canes distilled, a hot hellish and terrible liquor'. Very soon rumbullion was commonly abbreviated to rum and in 1654 the General Court of Connecticut ordered the confiscation of 'whatsoever Barbados liquors, commonly called Rum, Kill Devill or the like'.

A number of theories have been put forward as to the origin of the name. According to one authority, it comes from the Arabic; according to another, it is an abbreviation of *saccharum*, a Latin word for sugar. Such theories can be rejected out of hand, because they disregard the fact that rum is an abbreviation of rumbullion or rumbustion (both words were in use) and that the first recorded use of the name was in Barbados. It is a fairly safe assumption that the name was coined, not by the planters but in the Bridgetown taverns or on the Bridgetown waterfront, where the product was sold to foreign ships. Rumbullion may therefore have been an onomatopoeic or descriptive word, just as kill-devil was – after all, we still have the word rumbustious.

There is another possibility, which hitherto seems to have been overlooked. The word 'rummer', meaning a large drinking glass, is the English version of the Dutch and German word 'roemer', which was in common use long before the word rumbullion was invented. In the 1640s Barbados had a very close association with the Dutch and as Dutch seamen would undoubtedly have been heavy consumers of the spirit, it is by no means impossible that they coined a name for it and that the Barbadians Anglicized it.

Barbados was not, of course, the first country in which the spirit which we now call rum was made. It is, however, almost certainly the country where the name rum was invented and from which the product was first exported. For this reason it can claim with some justification to be the country where the rum industry of the Caribbean had its genesis.

The Development of an Export Market

When the Barbadians first started making rum it does not seem to have occurred to them that it had potential as an export product. Rum only became known abroad because ships visiting the island found that they could sell it in their home ports. No doubt some must have been sold in places such as Amsterdam and Hamburg, but in Holland and Germany there were other cheap spirits available and rum never got a foothold. It was in North America, where there was little competition, that Barbados rum found a ready sale.

Ships from New England and Virginia were bringing goods to Barbados almost as soon as the island was settled, but Barbados had little to offer in return. When Barbados started to make sugar the trade with North America expanded enormously. Barbados needed hogsheads and puncheons for its sugar, rum and molasses and North America became virtually the only source of supply. Before long it was also supplying most of the island's requirements of such items as fish, flour, beef and pork, livestock, dairy products and lumber. In return it took some sugar and molasses, but, most of all, it took rum. This was the cheapest form of alcohol available and it was immensely popular with people such as fishermen, lumberjacks and fur traders who led an outdoor life in the harsh northern winters. The Indians, too, could never get enough of it.

The Quality of Rum is Improved

The rum which was sold and consumed in the early years was in its raw state; it was extremely strong and it had a taste which most people found unpleasant. This was not altogether due to the method of manufacture; rum only becomes acceptable to more refined palates when it is reduced in strength by the addition of water and then left to mature in wooden casks. We do not know when the practice of maturing rum began, but some rum was probably being matured, perhaps for quite a short time, by about 1660.

The best known rum drink is rum punch. It consists of rum and sugar and the juice of lemons or limes. This mixture is diluted with water, but later on in Barbados we hear of milk punch, in which milk was substituted for water. The word 'punch' was in use in England before the English had ever seen rum. It was the same as rum punch except that it was made with wine or brandy. A Swiss doctor who visited Barbados in 1661 found that though punch was sometimes made with rum, 'the gentlemen of the island' preferred one, which they called 'lime drink', made with madeira wine. This was the well known Barbados drink later known as sangaree and was immensely popular in the island until well into the nineteenth century.

In England there is mention of rum punch houses as early as 1678, but there cannot have been more than one or two of them, because the total quantity of rum imported into England at that time was very small. It was not until about fifty years later that rum punch houses became common.

Competition in North America

Very early in the eighteenth century there was a development which caused the West Indian rum industry serious concern. Sugar cane must be processed immediately it is reaped, thus ensuring that sugar is made in the country where it is grown. The molasses from which rum is made can be kept for a long time without deteriorating. About the year 1700 it occurred to somebody in New England that it would be more profitable to import molasses and distil it than to import rum. What made this more attractive was there was cheap molasses available from the French islands, where much of it was being thrown away, because France prohibited the importation of rum in order to protect French brandy.

The distillation of rum from imported molasses began in Boston and Rhode Island and it soon spread to other American ports. Fortunately for Barbados, the rum was not nearly as good as West Indian rum; as one New Englander explained, 'it is not of the rum stink'.

Competition from American-distilled rum was serious but not disastrous. By this time the quality of the rum offered by Barbados and some of the other islands had greatly improved. A little later on, for example, we hear of Barbados and Jamaica making some of their rum from sugar cane juice instead of from molasses. It was called 'sugar cane juice' and fetched a higher price and it is said that the Barbados product was preferred. West Indian rum therefore retained the steadily expanding top end of the market, as well as a share of the lucrative West African trade. According to official statistics, the British islands were still supplying North America with three million gallons a year on the eve of the American Revolution.

We happen to know that Barbados rum was the choice of the first President of the United States. In 1751 George Washington brought his half-brother Lawrence to Barbados for his health. George spent seven weeks in the island and his diary records that he received much hospitality, so that no doubt he acquired a taste for Barbados rum. Many years later, when he first stood for election to the Virginian House of Burgesses, in accordance with the custom of the time he provided refreshment for the voters in his constituency. We are told that this included 40 gallons of rum punch and a hogshead and a barrel of the best Barbados rum.

England Takes to Rum

Imports of rum into England in 1698 amounted to 207 gallons. Seventy-five years later England and Ireland imported more than three and a half million gallons in a single year. Clearly the English and the Irish had acquired a taste for rum. How did this come about?

In the first half of the eighteenth century gin drinking among the lower classes reached alarming proportions; by 1742 gin consumption was twenty million gallons a year. In spite of this, a pamphlet published in London in the same year was referring to 'the prevailing taste for rum'. Rum punch was the fashionable

drink of London society; it was served at their dinner tables (which was not the case in Barbados) and it was consumed in taverns and punch houses. As early as 1715 we hear of it being supplied to voters at Parliamentary elections.

All this was good business, but it was making little impression on gin sales. It was a succession of bad grain harvests which caused the spectacular upsurge in English rum consumption. The Government was forced to prohibit the distillation of grain spirit and, though the prohibition was withdrawn three years later, rum had been introduced to a wider drinking public and had become well established. The West Indian planters and merchants reacted to the increased demand by raising their prices, but they still sold all they could produce.

The Golden Age of Rum

It was in the third quarter of the eighteenth century that sales of rum reached their peak. What that peak was, it is difficult to say. Occasionally figures are quoted for the production or the exports of a particular country and there are trade statistics of imports into Great Britain and North America, but the figures are often difficult to reconcile and, at best, they only give part of the picture. In the following paragraphs we shall attempt to construct a balance sheet based on the best information available.

Unless molasses is imported – and apparently it was not at this time – the amount of rum which can be produced is directly related to the amount of sugar which is made. Mainly because of weather conditions, this varied from year to year. There are, however, two ways in which rum production can be increased. The first is to convert the cane juice directly into rum, thereby, of course, reducing the tonnage of sugar. The second is to make rum of a lower strength. In Jamaica this was not possible because the law required all rum to be gauged to ensure that it was not below a certain strength. The Barbados Legislature refused to pass such a law and there were frequent complaints, in particular from North American customers, that the rum supplied was too weak. In Barbados these complaints fell on deaf ears. The demand for rum was so great that the island could sell all it could make.

The principal export markets in this period were Great Britain, Ireland and North America. Sales to these markets increased considerably after the passing of an Act by the British Parliament in 1764 prohibiting the importation of rum into British territories from foreign countries. Great Britain, for example, imported less than a million gallons in 1760 and an average of 2.3 million gallons in the years 1771–75. On the eve of the American Revolution imports into Great Britain and Ireland were 3.2 million gallons and into North America almost 3 million gallons.

These markets accounted for about two thirds of the estimated production of the British Caribbean. Who consumed the balance? Much of it was consumed in the Caribbean itself. In 1772 a Jamaican writer said that over a million and a half gallons were sold in the island and that most of it (1.2 million gallons) was drunk by slaves. In Barbados, about the same time, domestic consumption is given as 700,000 gallons – very much more than it is today. Domestic consumption of the British Caribbean as a whole cannot have been less than two and a half million gallons.

Though there was no direct export of rum to the continent of Europe, except in so far as visiting ships bought rum and re-sold it, this did not apply to the West African trade. West Africa had always been a good market for rum. Apart from sales to the population, rum was an important commodity in the barter trade for slaves and every slave ship carried a good supply. After 1700 some of this business was lost to rum distilled in North America, but this can only have applied to ships visiting American ports. We cannot even make a guess at the amount of rum which found its way to West Africa.

Rum has always had a close association with the sea. Originally, the drink that was carried on ships was beer, but on long voyages this went sour. Ships visiting Caribbean ports therefore took on board whatever was available and from the middle of the seventeenth century this was rum.

When Admiral Vernon, nicknamed Old Grog because of the grogram coat which he wore, was the British naval commander in the West Indies, he found that each member of a ship's crew was being issued with half a pint of neat rum a day. He also found that there was a great deal of drunkenness, though of course this was partly because the men were drinking heavily in the taverns on shore. He could not control what the men drank on shore, but he could do something about rum consumption on board. What he did do was to issue an order that in future the rum should be diluted with water and that half the daily allowance should be issued in the morning and half in the evening. This became the rum ration in all ships of the Royal Navy and was only discontinued in 1970. The ration became known as grog.

A great deal of rum must have been sold to the Royal Navy and as ships stores. We do not know the amount, but an incident which occurred some years earlier is of interest. When a naval squadron arrived in Jamaica in 1726 it found that the local rum, though ten per cent stronger, was much more expensive than rum from Barbados and the Leeward Islands. However, in order to protect local producers, the Jamaican Government had prohibited the importation of rum, even from other British colonies. When efforts to get this prohibition waived for rum imported for use by the navy were unsuccessful, the Government Victualler imported 100,000 gallons of rum from Barbados and claimed that the British Government was entitled to import it free of duty for official use. This claim was upheld by the British Law Officers.

With the advantage of hindsight, we can see that the Barbados planters were short-sighted. There were some people in Barbados who realized that the day would come when the rum export market would become competitive and that those islands whose rum had acquired a bad name because of its low strength would suffer. The crisis came in the 1770s as a result of a development which was completely unexpected.

Decline and Revival

In 1775 the American colonies rose in revolt against the mother

country and for the next eight years America and Great Britain were at war. Almost overnight, the West Indies lost a market for three million gallons of rum a year. England still wanted rum, but now that the commodity was in free supply she was free to choose her source of supply and the stronger rum from Jamaica was preferred. Within a few years rum imports into England from Barbados had dropped to less than half a million gallons. Business with America was resumed on a much reduced scale when a peace treaty was signed in 1783, but in 1812 Britain and the United States were again at war. This marked the virtual end of Barbados exports of rum to America for more than a century. The Americans now had their own corn spirit which was protected by a high import duty.

By the 1830s, for reasons still to be explained, Barbados had virtually ceased to be an exporter of rum; indeed, there were years in which she actually imported it. Production, which in the eighteenth century had reached two and a quarter million gallons, levelled off to about 400,000 gallons by the middle of the nineteenth. It is true that some molasses was now exported, but this was small compensation for the loss of rum sales.

It was not until the 1939–45 war that the Barbados rum export business revived. On the outbreak of war, exports amounted to less than 100,000 gallons, almost all of it going to the United Kingdom and Bermuda. By 1945, 1.3 million gallons of rum were being exported, with the United Kingdom, Trinidad and Canada (in that order) as the largest customers. Today Barbados rum is well established in markets such as Canada, the United States, the United Kingdom and Australia, as well as in some of the Caribbean countries.

History of Hanschell/ Cockspur

Hanschell Inniss Ltd., the blenders and bottlers of COCKSPUR, Barbados' most popular family of rums, was founded one hundred years ago, in 1884, by a Dane, Valdemar Hanschell. Cockspur Rum has been an integral part of the Company ever since. It has received acclaim at International Competition, winning Gold Awards for excellence on more than one occasion.

This success at home and abroad has been achieved through careful long-range planning. The consistent quality, for which COCKSPUR is famous, is guaranteed by the ever-growing reserves of hundreds of thousands of gallons of rum slowly

maturing in oaken casks, the largest reserves, by far, on the island.

Hanschell Inniss Ltd. presently offers four different COCKSPUR blends. There's Five Star, "the rum most Bajans prefer", available in coloured and white versions, Old Gold which is a blend of somewhat older rums and the very prestigious V.S.O.R. (Very Special Old Reserve), of which only limited supplies are available each year. Five Star, in particular, is full enough in flavour and body for use in traditional rum drinks and for culinary purposes, yet at the same time is sufficiently light and dry to be used in mixed drinks, cocktails or simply 'on the rocks'.

COCKSPUR is a great favourite in several of the Caribbean islands and is also exported to many countries, including the USA, Canada, Australia, Great Britain and Germany.

Daiquiri

Daiquiri is a refreshing drink which often contains fruit. Usually white rum is used in a daiquiri, but this is not essential.

Frozen Daiquiri

In a blender place
6 oz white rum
1 tbsp fresh lime juice
2 tbsp sugar
either
½ a very ripe banana
or
⅓ cup tinned mango or pineapple
2 cups ice
Blend until the final consistency is like snow.

Passion Daiquiri

1½ oz white rum
1 tbsp passion fruit juice
Juice of 1 lime
1 tsp sugar
Shake with ice and strain into a cocktail glass.

Cockspur Daiquiri

2½ oz Cockspur white rum
¼ oz lime juice
2 tsp sugar
3 ice cubes
Shake and strain into a cocktail glass.

Banana Daiquiri

Juice of half a lime
1 tsp sugar
Chopped banana
1½ oz white rum
Shake and blend with ice.

Bee's Kiss

1½ oz white rum
1 tbsp black coffee
1 tbsp fresh cream
Shake and blend with ice.

Cocktails

Rum forms the basis for many cooling cocktails. A few favourites are included here for you to shake and serve at almost any hour of the day or night. Golden rum is generally preferred.

Bossa Nova

4 parts golden rum
1 part lemon juice
1 part lime juice
2 parts passion fruit juice

Shake well and strain into a medium-sized glass. Serve with crushed ice and decorate with slices of orange and lime.

Mai-Tai

2 oz Cockspur golden rum
1 oz Curaçao
$\frac{1}{2}$ tsp sugar
1 tbsp Orgeat or almond-flavoured syrup
1 tbsp Grenadine

Shake with ice and strain into a large glass about $\frac{1}{3}$ full of crushed ice. Decorate with a cherry speared to a wedge of fruit, preferably fresh pineapple. Serve with a small straw.

Barbados Rum Cocktail

$1\frac{1}{2}$ oz golden rum
2 dashes Angostura bitters
Sugar to taste
Crushed ice
Shake together really well and strain into a glass.

Pineapple Cocktail

$1\frac{1}{2}$ oz golden rum
$\frac{3}{4}$ oz pineapple juice
$\frac{1}{2}$ tsp lemon juice
Shake with ice and strain into a cocktail glass.

Rum Sour

2 oz golden rum
$\frac{1}{2}$ tsp sugar
Juice of $\frac{1}{2}$ lemon
Shake with ice and strain into a glass. Garnish with half a slice of lemon and a cherry.

Spanish Town Cocktail

2 oz white rum
1 tsp Triple Sec
Stir with ice and strain into cocktail glasses.

Yellow Bird

$1\frac{1}{2}$ oz golden rum
3 oz pineapple juice
$\frac{1}{4}$ oz orange juice
$\frac{3}{4}$ oz Creme de Banana
Dash of Galliano
$\frac{1}{4}$ oz apricot brandy
Shake well and serve in a tall glass.

Fruit & Rum

The sweet and sometimes sour taste of Caribbean fruits mixes particularly well with the richness of rum.

Pineapple Caribbean

1 pineapple
3 cubes ice
1 oz vodka
1 oz Cockspur golden rum
½ oz apricot brandy
½ oz cherry brandy
1 dash Angostura bitters
12 Maraschino cherries
Lemon slices
1 olive

Slice top off pineapple about 2″ from top. Hollow out the pineapple and cut half the fruit into small cubes. Place fruit back in pineapple. Into cocktail shaker put ice cubes, vodka, rum, apricot brandy, cherry brandy and bitters and shake. Pour unstrained over the fruit in the pineapple shell. Place 4 toothpicks around the edge of the pineapple shell and thread 3 cherries on to each toothpick. Place 4 toothpicks in lid of pineapple to correspond with position of bottom toothpicks. Place lid back so that toothpicks go into the cherries. Decorate with 2 slices (round) of lemon, ¼″ thick, one slice on either side of pineapple. Balance two crossed swizzle sticks on toothpick that goes through the lemon. Secure the sticks by placing an olive on the exposed part of the toothpick. Serve with a spoon and drinking straws.

Rum Daisy

⅓ glass white rum
Juice of ½ lemon
1 tbsp Grenadine
Cherries
Bananas

Shake the liquid ingredients together and decorate with cherries and bananas.

Highballs

Traditionally, highballs are the most thirst quenching drinks served in a tall glass with plenty of ice. Best with golden or white rum.

Rum Screwdriver

$1\frac{1}{2}$ oz Cockspur white rum
Orange juice
Ice cubes
Pour the orange juice over the ice cubes and top with the rum measure.

Rum Highball

$1\frac{1}{2}$ oz golden rum
Ice cubes
Ginger ale
Put all the ingredients into a tall glass and garnish with zest of lemon or orange.

Durkee Highball-soda

$1\frac{1}{2}$ oz golden rum
1 tbsp Triple Sec
1 tsp sugar syrup
Soda water
Ice cubes
Shake the rum, Triple Sec and sugar syrup together thoroughly with ice. Strain into a glass and top up with soda water.

Rum Rickey

$1\frac{1}{2}$ oz golden rum
Juice of $\frac{1}{2}$ lime
Soda water
Pour the lime juice into a tall glass containing ice cubes, add the rum and top up with soda water.

Rum Collins

$1\frac{1}{2}$ oz white or golden rum
2 tsp sugar
Juice of 1 lemon
Fizzy orangeade
Ice cubes
Dash of Angostura bitters
Pour all the ingredients into a tall glass, garnish with a slice of orange, a cherry and a piece of banana.

Juleps

There are many julep recipes – most of them include plenty of crushed ice and a generous garnish of mint sprigs and fresh fruit.

Rum Julep

1½ oz white rum
3 sprigs mint
1 tsp sugar
1 tbsp water
Lightly crush the mint with the sugar and water. Add rum and garnish with mint leaves.

Rum Mojito
The famous Cuban drink

2 oz white rum
¼ oz lemon juice
1 tsp sugar
Several ice cubes
Soda water
2 drops Angostura bitters
Mint leaves
Stir sugar and lemon juice well, add the rum and ice. Top the glass up with soda water, add bitters and garnish with mint leaves.

Pina Colada

Possibly one of the most famous Caribbean rum drinks.

Pina Colada is a classic

1½ oz Cockspur white rum
1 oz cream of coconut
3 oz unsweetened pineapple juice
1 cup crushed ice

Combine all the ingredients in a blender for 10 to 20 seconds. Serve in a tall glass, with a straw, and garnish with pineapple.

Punches

Another popular family of drinks. A good rum punch should be a subtle blend of flavours, well mixed and attractively presented. Golden rum makes the best punch.

Party Punch

16 oz orange juice
16 oz pineapple juice
16 oz Club soda
16 oz rum
Sugar to taste
3 oz lime juice
Pour all the ingredients into a large punch bowl with crushed ice.

Planter's Punch

3 parts rum
1 part lime juice
2 parts sugar syrup
3 parts water
Dash of Curaçao or
Angostura bitters
Combine all the ingredients and serve in tall glasses with cherries and orange slices and plenty of ice.

Pirates Punch

2 parts golden rum
1 part sweet vermouth
Dash of Angostura bitters
Shake well with ice and strain into a glass.

Carlisle Rum Punch

½ pint strained lime juice
¼ pint strained orange juice
¼ pint strained pineapple juice
2 tbsp sugar syrup
2 or 3 dashes Angostura bitters
Cherries
¾ pint golden rum
Cracked ice
Grated nutmeg
Halved pineapple slices
Orange slices

Mix all ingredients except ice and fruit in a bowl. Half fill cups with cracked ice, fill up with punch, sprinkle with nutmeg and float pineapple and orange slices and cherries on top.

Rum & One

Simple rum drinks have a clear and crisp flavour. Here are some suggestions for rum and one mixes. Why not conjure up some of your own? Use golden or white rum for preference.

Teatotaller

1 part iced tea
1 part rum
Stir the tea and rum together with ice and serve in tall glasses.

Rum and Tonic

1½ oz rum poured on ice, topped with tonic water and garnished with a slice of lemon or lime.

Rum and Coke

1½ oz rum poured on ice and topped up with Coke.

Rum Gimlet

Pour 1½ oz rum over ice into a cocktail glass. Add ½ oz lime juice cordial and decorate with a slice of fresh lime.

White Rum

Drinks made with white rum are naturally mellow yet refreshing.

Rum Martini

4–5 ice cubes
1 part dry vermouth
3 parts Cockspur white rum
1 slice fresh lemon rind

Put the ice cubes into a glass jug, pour the vermouth and rum over the ice. Stir vigorously, strain into a chilled martini glass. Twist the fresh lemon rind over the drink and drop it in.

Naked Lady

1½ oz white rum
1½ oz sweet vermouth
4 dashes apricot brandy
2 dashes Grenadine
4 dashes lemon juice

Shake well with ice and strain into a cocktail glass.

Rum Bloody Mary

1½ oz white rum
4–5 oz tomato juice
Squeeze of fresh lemon
Dash of Tabasco sauce
Dash of Worcester sauce

Shake well and strain into a wineglass. Add salt and freshly ground black pepper to taste.

Hot Rum

The smooth and soothing taste of these hot rum recipes will warm you during the cooler winter evenings. Golden rum is your first choice here.

Hot Punch

1 tbsp powdered ginger
3 pints warmed beer
3 eggs
¼ pint golden rum
1 tsp grated nutmeg
2 tbsp molasses

Blend the ginger and nutmeg with 2½ pints beer and heat. Beat the eggs with the remaining beer and molasses. Add the warm beer to the egg mixture a little at a time, beating all the time. Add the rum and serve at once.

Cafe Calypso (Hot)

4 cups freshly percolated coffee
8 tbsp Cockspur golden rum
12 tbsp coffee liqueur
¼ pint whipped cream

Blend the coffee liqueur and rum gently with the coffee in a heat-proof jug. The coffee should be hot but not boiling. Serve the drink in large coffee cups, or brandy snifters, sweetening slightly with castor sugar and top with whipped cream.

Hot Rum Toddy

Put 2 oz golden rum in a mug with one tsp sugar and add 3 oz of hot water and stir well. Add a twist of lemon or orange peel.

Special Hot Barbadian Rum Punch

1 bottle rum	1 bottle brandy
2 lemons	½ bottle sherry
4 oz sugar	1 tsp ginger
Up to 3½ pints boiling water	Grated nutmeg

Grate the rind of the lemons into a small earthenware bowl and add sugar. Macerate sugar and lemon gratings, add the juice of lemons and ginger. Mix well and place in another large earthenware bowl previously heated. Then add, in the following order, rum, brandy, sherry and boiling water. Mix well, sweeten further if desired and stand near heat for 20 minutes before serving in glasses or mugs with a grating of nutmeg on top.

Hot Rum and Chocolate

Add 2 oz golden rum to a cup of hot chocolate and top with whipped cream.

Cooking with Rum

Cooking with rum offers many opportunities to prepare enjoyable dishes. The addition of rum provides a special quality to enhance almost any meal. It can be added to soups and the dressings for salads, to main courses such as steak and chicken, and to desserts whether mousses, souffles or cakes. A very small number of recipes are included here as examples of how rum can be used to delight the palate.

Chocolate Rum Mousse

1 pkt chocolate chips
2 tbsp water
2 tbsp rum
5 eggs

Melt chocolate chips over low heat. Stir in rum. Separate eggs and beat chocolate mixture into the yolks. Beat egg whites separately and fold in. Pour into custard cups and chill for at least 4 hours.
Serves 8.

Caribbean fruits in rum

2 tangerines
3 mangoes
1 lb strawberries, hulled
½ pineapple, peeled and diced
2 inch stick cinnamon
2 lb brown sugar
2 lb granulated sugar
1½ pints rum

Peel tangerines, removing all the pith, divide into segments and discard pips. Peel mangoes, remove stones and slice. Put the fruits in a large bowl with the cinnamon stick. Add the sugars and toss the fruit. Set aside for 1 hour turning the fruit over three or four times to ensure even distribution of the sugar.

Cockspur Rum Coffee Cake

8 inch ring shape cake tin or 8 inch diameter deep cake tin

4 oz butter
4 oz sugar
2 eggs
1–2 drops vanilla essence
4 oz self-raising flour
Pinch of salt
½ fluid oz cold strong black coffee
2 fluid oz Cockspur golden rum
½ pint double or whipping cream
6 oz walnuts – chopped coarsely

Beat together butter and sugar until lemon coloured, light and fluffy. Very gradually beat in the eggs, beating thoroughly between each addition. Add the vanilla essence. Sieve flour and salt, and fold into the mixture. Turn into well greased cake tin and bake in moderate oven (180°C, Gas Mark 4) for 30–35 minutes.

Turn cake out of tin and allow to cool. When completely cold, turn back into tin and stab with fork or skewer at ½ inch intervals all round the cake. Pour coffee and rum over and allow to soak for at least 1–2 hours.

Whip cream until it just holds its shape. Turn cake out onto serving dish and cover with cream. Scatter with walnuts. Serves 8.